The Extraordinary
Book That Eats Itself

Written by Susan Hayes and Penny Arlon
Illustrated by Pintachan

CUT UP THIS BOOK! It is reusable or recyclable—every little bit of it!

EARTHAWARE
KIDS

A Message from Dr Amy Dickman
Conservationist and wildlife expert

Thank you for reading The Extraordinary Book That Eats Itself! We live in such a beautiful world filled with incredible wildlife, from powerful lions to fascinating insects. We have rich forests, brilliant birds, amazing oceans, and so much else—we are so lucky to call this planet our home.

Unfortunately, the world has problems, including too much waste. By enjoying this book, and using it for environmentally friendly projects, you will have fun, avoid waste, and help our amazing planet!

This book is really unusual in that every single bit of it is designed to be used in fun, eco-friendly activities. Our planet is facing some big issues, like climate change and plastic pollution. But my work in Africa has shown me that if you get people to join together and make small changes, together we can make a huge difference.

That is why you using this book is so important—by learning about the planet and doing small things to help, you will create a better future for our wonderful Earth and its people and wildlife. So, please start your projects, and have fun while helping our environment!

Amy is fighting to save African lions from extinction. She works with local people to protect lions and other wildlife, and with other conservationists to look after the environment.

CONTENTS

Welcome to The Extraordinary Book That Eats Itself!

1 Build a worm bin to recycle your food scraps

2 Pass and share to reduce buying and wasting

3 Go plastic free to stop harming ocean creatures

4 Grow your own to save food miles

5 Turn it down to save electricity

6 Turn off the lights to stop light pollution

7 Upcycle your junk to reduce wasle and save landfill space

8 Have an eco-picnic that doesn't harm the planet

9 Plant a tree to help slow down global warming

10 Adopt a wild animal to protect its home

11 Recycle garbage to make musical instruments

12 Plant an apple tree to help save the bees

13 Have a litter pickup to clean up our shared spaces

14 Chase away vampires to save electric power in your home

15 Build a bug hotel to protect the mini-recyclers

RECYCLE THIS PAGE! Use it to make a seed tray for project 12.

16 **Sort and recycle** to reduce landfill

17 **Plant wild seeds** to save the butterflies

18 **Bike or hike** instead of using the car

19 **Feed the birds** to keep our ecosystem healthy

20 **Swap, mix, and match** to recycle your clothes

21 **Save water** to make sure we all have enough

22 **Buy less plastic** to stop polluting our planet

23 **Throw a seedball** to reseed the landscape

24 **Make a difference** in your own home

25 **Rescue old clothes** to reuse the fabric

26 **Make your own pizza** without chemicals or food miles

27 **Avoid plastic** to stop harming our animals

28 **Eat up** to stop food waste

29 **Spread the word** to help save the planet

30 **Don't forget** to recycle the cover and the cover flaps!

RECYCLE THIS PAGE! Use it to make a seed tray for project 12.

WELCOME to
The Extraordinary Book That Eats Itself

Most books are just meant to be read.
But this is no ordinary book.

This is a book that turns itself into dozens of eco-projects to inspire you to think more about the planet we all call home.

Do you want to be good at reducing, reusing, and recycling?

This book doesn't just want you to read about it.

The Extraordinary Book That Eats Itself asks you to DO something about it, too.

You can cut up, fold, tear, and reuse every single page (even the cover) to make all sorts of interesting projects—from planters and seed writing papers to eco-badges.

There are eco-quizzes and nature games, growing projects and organic recipes, bug hotels, and plastic-free diaries.

And don't forget to make the eco-friendly glue with the recipe on the back cover flap!

DON'T FORGET TO RECYCLE THIS PAGE! Use it to make some bug hotel rooms for project 15.

There are many activities to do on your own, and others to try with an adult's help—all of which can help you to change the way you think about the natural world and how you can make a real difference.

And don't worry if what you do seems small.

If everyone joins in with lots of small actions, together we can make a BIG difference!

Are you ready to start?

Just follow the steps on the opposite page to make a mini worm bin.

Then, carefully pull out the page along the spine, and turn it into a worm bin cover to keep your wriggly friends cool, dark, and damp.

If you and your family like the idea, you might decide to make a giant worm bin to recycle ALL your food scraps.

Little by little, **The Extraordinary Book That Eats Itself** is your guide to taking action!

BUILD A WORM BIN
to recycle your food scraps

1
Turn over to make a worm bin cover.

Instead of putting your food scraps into landfill, send in the worms! Recycle in a healthy, green way.

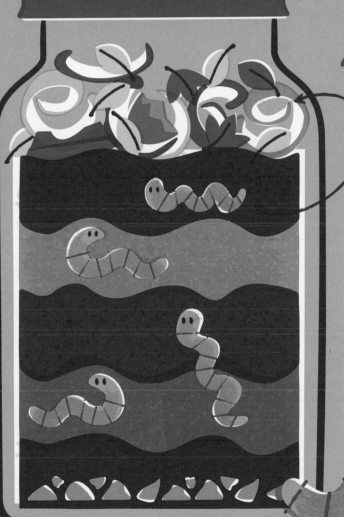

Holes let the worms breathe.

The worms eat the leaves and peelings.

Release the worms after a couple of days.

You will need

¼ cup gravel

empty jar with lid

soil

1 tbsp water

sand

leaves, vegetable peelings

earthworms

Now talk to your family about making a bigger worm bin. Composting ALL your scraps will make a difference.

Make a mini worm bin

1 Put gravel into the bottom of a small, thin jar. Add a layer of soil and then sand.

2 Layer more soil and sand. Drip a little water over the top.

3 Add three or four worms, a few leaves, and some vegetable scraps.

4 Ask an adult to help make some holes in the jar lid. Twist it on.

5 Keep the jar cool and dark. Use the other side of this page as a wrap.

Wrap this sheet around your worm bin to keep it dark and cool. Cut the slits and slide together to hold in place.

PASS AND SHARE
to reduce buying and wasting

2

Turn over to cut out a bookmark to share.

Invite friends to bring over a game, then swap.

Next time you are about to throw something away, think first. Who might use that? Swap books, toys, and games with friends to avoid buying too many new things. Recycling is fun and helps save the planet.

Grown out of those boots? Pass them on!

Pass a book on with a special bookmark inside.

Escape into my favorite book!

Read this. Let's compare notes!

Get lost . . . in this terrific tale!

Leap into this amazing story!

Relax and enjoy this awesome book!

Get ready for goose bumps in this thriller!

GO PLASTIC FREE
to stop harming ocean creatures

3
Turn over to take the plastic-free challenge.

Sadly, turtles often think plastic looks and smells like food and eat it.

Millions of tons of plastic are washed into oceans from rivers and beaches. Avoid plastic to keep our wildlife safe.

When a whale gulps water to catch fish it catches plastic too, which blocks its gut.

Five ways to avoid using plastic

1 Don't buy plastic bottles. Fill up a reusable one with water instead.

2 Take a reusable bag shopping to save you from buying a plastic one.

3 Say NO to plastic straws. Use a paper one or use no straw at all!

4 Ask your family to buy fruit and vegetables with no plastic packaging.

5 Pack a plastic-free lunch. Remember, no plastic wrap or plastic baggies!

Take the plastic-free challenge!

Put up this checklist in your home.

✓ YES!	✗ NO!
Bamboo toothbrush	Plastic toothbrush
Soap bar	Liquid soap in a plastic bottle
Loose vegetables	Plastic tub of vegetables
Reusable bag	Throwaway bag
Paper straw	Plastic straw
Reusable bottles	Plastic bottles

You can make a difference
and help the ocean creatures!

✂ -

WEEK 1 plastic checklist

Plastic item	How many in your home?
toothbrush	....
soap bottles	....
bags	....
straws	....
tubs	....
bottles	....

Count the plastic items.
Can you make a difference?

WEEK 4 plastic checklist

Plastic item	How many in your home?
toothbrush	....
soap bottles	....
bags	....
straws	....
tubs	....
bottles	....

Count again four weeks later.
Did you make a difference?

GROW YOUR OWN
to save food miles

4 Turn over to make homegrown strawberry treats.

Every day, fruit is taken from one place to another. All that travel releases harmful gases into the air.

In most countries, strawberries are only in season for a few months each year. The rest come from abroad. Grow your own to help keep the air clean.

Find out when is the best time to grow strawberries where you live.

Grow a strawberry bag!

You will need

strawberry plants

scissors

a canvas bag

compost

1 Ask an adult to help cut slits in the bottom and sides of the bag. Add compost.

2 At each slit, put in a plant, pushing the leaves out through the slits from inside.

3 Put the final two plants in the top, covering the roots with soil. Water well.

4 Keep the bag in a sunny spot and water regularly.

Strawberry Slushy

You will need

1 teaspoon sugar

3 ice cubes

juice of half a lemon

a sprig of mint

1 cup of strawberries

1 | Blend the strawberries, ice cubes, lemon juice, and sugar in a blender.

2 | Serve in your favorite glass and decorate with a sprig of mint!

Strawberry Milkshake

You will need

2 cups strawberries

1 tablespoon honey

1 ½ cups milk

1 | Put all the ingredients into a blender and blend.

2 | Pour into a glass and add a strawberry on top.

Strawberries and Cream

You will need

strawberries

whipped cream

sugar

1 | Remove the leaves from the berries and cut in half.

2 | Put them into a bowl and add whipped cream.

3 | Sprinkle some sugar on top.

Strawberry Popsicles

You will need

½ cup strawberries

popsicle stick

1 teaspoon sugar

1 cup plain yogurt

1 | Blend the ingredients in a blender.

2 | Pour the mix into a reusable container. Add a popsicle stick.

3 | Freeze overnight. Pop it out to eat!

TURN IT DOWN
to save electricity

5
Turn over to make a cooling fan.

You don't always have to turn on the heating or air-conditioning. There are other ways to stay warm or cool that don't waste electricity.

Make a hot drink to warm yourself up.

Add ice to a cold drink to help keep cool.

Don't turn up the heat

| Wear an extra-thick sweater and socks instead.

2 Make sure you close windows to keep out drafts.

Don't turn on the air-conditioning

| Keep blinds closed to block out the sun's heat.

2 Use a handmade fan to keep yourself cool.

Make a cooling fan

1 Cut out the fan base above. Fold along the first line.

2 Turn over and fold the same amount on the other side.

3 Keep turning over and folding until you reach the end.

4 Squeeze one end together and fan yourself cool.

5 Look at the fan from each side. Can you see the two pictures?

DON'T THROW THIS AWAY! Keep the instructions to make another fan from recycled paper.

TURN OFF THE LIGHTS
to stop light pollution

6
Turn over to send out reminder notices.

Lights glow above cities at night, lighting up the land. This confuses animals that need the darkness to keep safe.

Some animals use moonlight to find their way.

Lights should be turned off at night.

How city lights affect animals

Moths use light from the moon to help find their way. They get confused and fly toward city lights instead.

Tree frogs call out in the dark to find a mate. Too much light means they don't call and don't breed.

Voles use darkness to hide from predators. City lights make them easier to spot.

Turtles use moonlight to find the sea from the beach when they hatch. Some head toward city lights instead.

Pass on these messages to friends and family to ask them to turn their lights off at night. Use this notice to remind yourself.

To.....................................

Please remember to switch off office lights at night. Light pollution confuses animals.

To.....................................

Light at night wastes electricity and is dangerous for animals. Please switch off.

Save the animals! Help bring back darkness at night by turning your lights off.

To.....................................

Turn lights off to bring back dark nights. It's safer for animals.

To.....................................

Stop light pollution and stop wasting electricity. Please turn off the office lights at night.

To.....................................

Please switch off the lights. Keep the animals safe.

To.....................................

Keep our animals safe at night. Switch off the office lights when you leave.

UPCYCLE YOUR JUNK
to reduce waste and save landfill space

Don't throw away an old bike. Fix and repaint it.

Reuse old jars. It takes a million years for glass to rot away!

Recycling is good but upcycling is even better! Instead of throwing things away, turn them into something new.

Repair and decorate to give old things a new life.

Old boots make great flower pots!

Turn something old into something new

1 Don't throw away your favorite old things. Use pictures and glue to upcycle.

2 Turn over and cut out some fun pictures. Find more images in magazines.

3 Ask an adult to help you make the eco-friendly glue recipe on the back cover.

4 Use plenty of glue to stick the pictures on your "treasure."

5 Paste more glue over the pictures to make them strong. Leave to dry overnight.

HAVE AN ECO-PICNIC
that doesn't harm the planet

8

Turn over to make eco-picnic invitations.

1 Pick a local spot that you can walk or cycle to.

2 Pack a picnic with no plastic wraps.

3 Bring reusable drinks, bottles, and cutlery.

4 Invite your friends. Remind them to be eco-friendly, too.

5 Clean up and take your trash home.

You're invited to a
PICNIC PARTY
Date .... Time ....
Walk or cycle to ....
....
Please pack an
eco-friendly picnic!

You're invited to a
PICNIC PARTY
Date .... Time ....
Walk or cycle to ....
....
Please pack an
eco-friendly picnic!

You're invited to a
PICNIC PARTY
Date ....
Time ....
Walk or cycle to ....
....
Please pack an eco-friendly picnic!

You're invited to a
PICNIC PARTY
Date .... Time ....
Walk or cycle to ....
....
Please pack an
eco-friendly picnic!

You're invited to a
PICNIC PARTY
Date .... Time ....
Walk or cycle to ....
....
Please pack an
eco-friendly picnic!

You're invited to a
PICNIC PARTY
Date .... Time ....
Walk or cycle to ....
....
Please pack an
eco-friendly picnic!

PLANT A TREE
to help slow down global warming

9 Turn over to make garden markers.

If everyone on Earth planted just one tree, it would help global warming slow down.

Trees are amazing. They breathe in harmful carbon dioxide and turn it into oxygen.

Trees are also homes for wildlife.

Tree roots keep the soil stable, which helps to stop flooding.

Plant a sapling

 1 Put some gravel at the bottom of a pot. Fill it with soil.

 2 Push the seed half a finger length into the soil. Water it so the soil is damp.

 3 Keep the pot outside in a shady corner. Water it once a week.

 4 As the plant grows bigger, replant it into bigger pots.

 5 Plant it in your garden, or ask to plant in a forest or park. Watch it grow!

I'm a planet hero by growing this.............tree!

I'm zapping global warming by growing this.............tree!

I'm crushing carbon by growing this.............tree!

I'm cleansing our air by growing this.............tree!

I'm treasuring our Earth by growing this.............tree!

I'm hugging our planet by growing this.............tree!

ADOPT A WILD ANIMAL
to protect its home

10 Turn over to make an endangered tiger face.

Many animals are endangered. People can adopt to protect them. Ask an adult to help you research how you can help too.

Supporting a polar bear will protect it from being hunted.

By adopting a tiger, you can help stop its rain forest home from being cut down.

Make an origami tiger face to honor endangered animals

1 Turn over to cut out a paper square for your tiger origami.

2 Fold the paper in half with the tiger face at the top.

3 Turn over. Fold the left and right corners to the bottom point.

4 Turn up the bottom two flaps to make the ears.

5 Fold in the two flaps at the edge.

6 Turn the paper over so you can see the face.

7 Fold the bottom corner up to cover the nose.

8 Fold a small flap down to create the nose tip.

9 Fold back the triangle at the top behind the head.

10 Display the tiger to remind you to help the animals.

DON'T THROW THIS AWAY! Keep the instructions to make more endangered animal faces out of recycled paper.

RECYCLE GARBAGE
to make musical instruments

11

Turn over to make a trumpet.

Use a couple of old lids to bang as cymbals.

Don't throw away all your garbage. Turn it into something else. Make instruments and form a band!

Fill jars or bottles with buttons to make shakers.

Beat tin cans as drums.

Make jam jar music

1 Keep and wash out your old glass jars and bottles.

2 Fill each container with a different amount of water.

3 Tap the jars and bottles with a wooden spoon to create notes.

4 Make a colorful run of notes by filling each one with a different amount of colored water. Now you can play a tune!

Cut out these templates to make three trumpets.

glue here

glue here

Don't throw away all the little cutout bits.
Recycle them for other projects in this book!

Make trumpets for your recycled garbage band

1 Cut out the cone shapes above. Glue the ends together.

2 Cut out the tubes on the inside cover. Snip the slot lines.

3 Roll and glue each card into a tube. Bend the tabs back.

4 Slide each tube through a cone. Glue in place.

5 Now hand out your trumpets to your friends and jam!

DON'T THROW THIS AWAY! Save the instructions to make more trumpets out of recycled card.

PLANT AN APPLE TREE
to help save the bees

Apple trees grow best in a sunny, sheltered place.

Bees are very important. They help to pollinate a third of our crops. But over-building and over-farming mean that there is less land for the flowers that bees need to feed.

It's fun to grow an apple tree from seed. But it will take several years to produce apples.

Bees love apple blossoms. They take the sweet nectar and turn it into honey.

Fold a seed tray to plant apple seeds

1 Turn this page over to cut out the paper. Fold the paper and unfold.

2 Fold each corner to meet the center until you have a smaller square.

3 Fold the top and bottom sides to the center and unfold.

4 Open the top and bottom flaps. Fold the sides in to meet in the center.

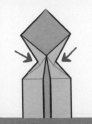

5 Pull both side openings down to pinch the triangles together.

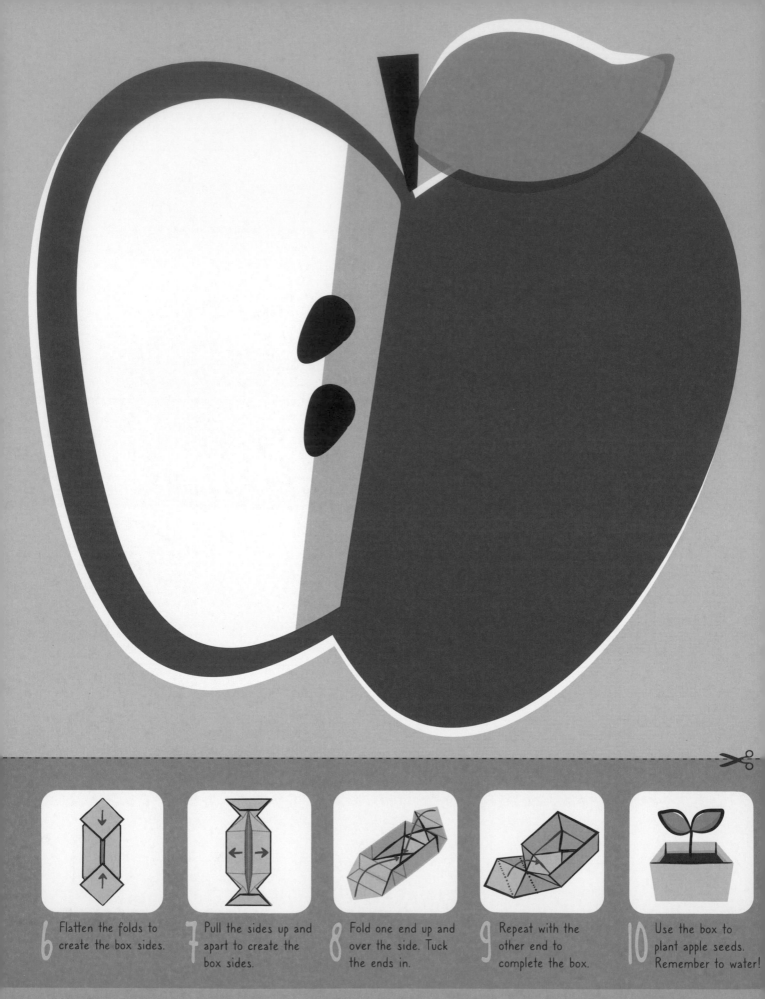

6 Flatten the folds to create the box sides.

7 Pull the sides up and apart to create the box sides.

8 Fold one end up and over the side. Tuck the ends in.

9 Repeat with the other end to complete the box.

10 Use the box to plant apple seeds. Remember to water!

DON'T THROW ME AWAY! Save these instructions to make another tray from recycled paper. You can plant all sorts of fruit seeds.

HAVE A LITTER PICKUP
to clean up our shared spaces

13
Turn over to make litter pickup invitations.

Litter heroes unite! We've only got one home so let's keep it clean. Host a litter pickup to stop polluting our planet.

Litter contains harmful chemicals that poison the Earth.

Wear protective clothing while picking up litter.

Invite your friends to a litter pickup

1 Choose a park, beach, or road in your area to pick up litter.

2 Put on your superhero litter gloves and boots.

3 Give everyone a collection bag to fill with litter.

4 Set your watches! Who can fill their bag first?

5 Sort through the litter to recycle as much as you can.

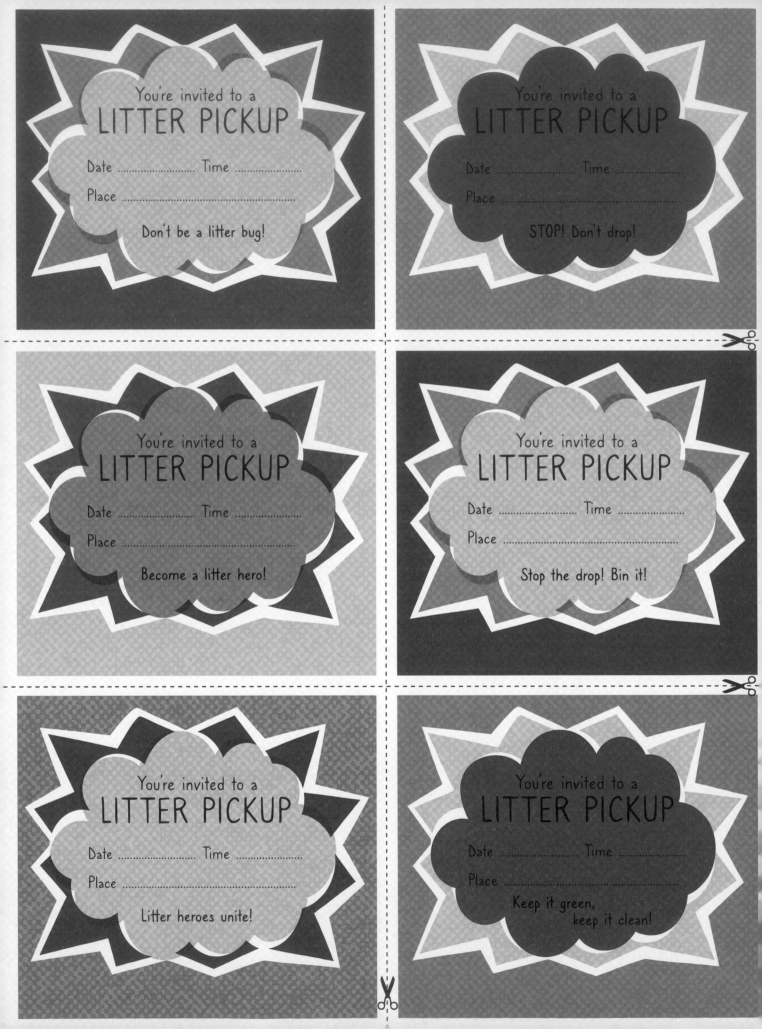

CHASE AWAY VAMPIRES
to save electric power in your home

HUNT THE RED-EYED MONSTER

WATCH OUT! There are vampires in your home! Vampires are electrical objects that suck power —even when you think you aren't using them.

One house could save as much as 10% of its electricity by cutting out the standby power.

Take control of your gadgets

1 If your TV has a red light on, it's using power. Turn it off at the outlet.

2 Check your game consoles, DVD players, and cable boxes too.

3 Turn off your computer and printer. Standby is still sucking.

4 Turn off digital clocks on microwaves and radios. They are still using power.

5 Unplug devices when they are charged. Don't plug them in all night.

BUILD A BUG HOTEL
to protect the mini-recyclers

15 Turn over to make "rooms" for your bug hotel.

Minibeasts help to pollinate flowers, and many recycle dead plants into soil again. Build them a safe home.

Bark chippings are great for ladybugs to hibernate in over winter.

Different materials attract different bugs.

Lacewings love to nest in rolled tubes.

! WARNING!
Do not touch the bug hotel once your guests have arrived. Some creatures can bite or sting.

You will need

leaves and grass
bark

large tin cans
pine cone

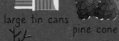

twigs
rolled paper tubes
dried moss

Make a bug hotel

1 Ask an adult to clean some large, used tin cans. Make sure there are no sharp edges.

2 Fill the tin cans with bark, twigs, pine cones, leaves, moss, or grass.

3 Turn over to make tubes for the lacewings. Use the inside front cover, too.

4 Stack the cans in a shady spot and wait for your bug hotel guests to arrive!

Cut out the rectangles,
including this one.
Roll them into tubes
for your bug hotel.

SORT AND RECYCLE
to reduce landfill

Ask an adult to repair electronics. If they can't, take them to a recycling center.

We don't need to throw everything into landfill. Recycle as much as you can. Think of ways to separate your trash.

Recycle paper. One ton saves 17 trees!

Recycle your clothing. Very little of our clothing is recycled when it all could be!

Compost your food scraps so they break down in a healthy way.

Have separate containers for different types of garbage. Turn over to cut out labels to put on each container.

PAPER

Save the trees, recycle paper.

APPLIANCES

Ask an adult to repair your electric appliances.

RAW FOOD SCRAPS

Set up a family compost.

BATTERIES

Take batteries to a recycling center.

GLASS

Reuse or recycle all glass.

CLOTHES

Give away your old clothes.

PLANT WILD SEEDS
to save the butterflies

17 Turn over to make a seed collection pouch.

When land is cleared to grow crops or build homes, flowers are lost. Wildflowers produce the nectar that butterflies drink.

Some butterflies help to pollinate by taking pollen from flower to flower.

Caterpillars and butterflies are important food for birds and small animals.

Find out which flowers attract butterflies and grow them in a pot.

Fold a seed collection pouch

1 Cut out the template above. Fold it in half.

2 Fold the bottom right corner up to the edge.

3 Repeat with the bottom left corner.

4 Tuck the front top triangle into the pocket.

5 Fill your pouch with wildflower seeds and fold the top down.

DON'T THROW THIS AWAY! Keep the instructions to make a pouch for next year's seeds.

BIKE OR HIKE
instead of using the car

18

Turn over to play the "I spy" game.

Next time you plan a family day out, leave the car at home! Cars give out harmful fumes that lead to global warming.

Walking and cycling don't harm the planet like cars and buses do.

Try to spot birds and other animals.

Check the weather first and wear the right clothes!

Don't forget to pack a reusable water bottle.

Play nature "I spy" on your day out

1 Cut out the "I spy" papers on the next page and put them into a jar.

2 Get each person on your bike or hike to pick out the same number of papers.

3 Search for the things on your pictures or anything beginning with the letters.

4 First to find them all, or whoever finds the most, is the winner!

5 Save the papers for another game on your next trip.

FEED THE BIRDS
to keep our ecosystem healthy

19
Turn over to fold an origami bird.

Hang up a pine cone feeder.

Birds keep control of pests by eating insects.

Birds help carry seeds to faraway places.

Many animals struggle to find food in winter or when land is cleared for building or farming. Feed the birds to help them thrive.

You will need

pine cone

string

food mix of bird seeds, raisins, and nuts

peanut butter or lard

‼ If you have a peanut allergy, use lard instead.

‼ Only use this feeder in the winter.

Make a pine cone feeder

1 Mix the peanut butter or the lard with the food mix until it all holds together.

2 Cut off a length of string and attach it to the top of the pine cone. Tie a knot.

3 Squash the mixture into the gaps in the pine cone. Hang it up outside for the birds.

Fold an origami bird

1 Cut out the bird paper. Fold it in half.

2 Fold the top part of the triangle down.

3 Turn over and fold the top flap up.

4 Fold the shape in half from left to right.

5 Now fold the right flap back to make a wing.

6 Turn over and fold the other wing back.

7 Fold a little triangle over for the beak.

8 Put your bird on display!

DON'T THROW ME AWAY! Save the instructions to make more paper birds from recycled paper. Display your origami to remind you to feed the birds.

SWAP, MIX, AND MATCH
to recycle your clothes

Don't throw away your old clothes. Throw a swap party instead! Mix, match, and swap to stop good clothes from wasting away in landfill.

Don't waste a hat that still has good wear in it!

Make a mix and match badge for your new outfit.

Grown out of a skirt? Give it away. Don't throw it away.

A truckload of clothes is dumped every second. Don't add to it!

Swap jeans —it takes 25 bathtubs of water to make a new pair.

It can take sneakers 1,000 years to decompose. Wear them out instead!

Wear a mix and match badge to encourage everyone to clothes swap

1 Cut the badge shapes out of the cover flap of this book.

2 Thread a safety pin through the two holes.

3 Cut out your mix of face parts and arrange a crazy face.

4 Use the homemade glue to stick the pieces down.

5 Wear your badge to show you're proud to mix and match.

DON'T THROW ME AWAY! Use these instructions to make more crazy badges out of recycled paper!

SAVE WATER
to make sure we all have enough

Less than one percent of the water on Earth is available to use. The rest is seawater or locked in ice.

Every drop of water we use must be cleaned afterward. This uses energy and electricity.

A dripping tap can waste a whole bathtub full of water in one day!

Water is precious. We need to drink it to survive, and we use it in our homes and factories. Save water to keep it clean and plentiful.

How can I save water?

Look after our water by using less. Every drop counts!

1 Turn off the water while you brush your teeth.

2 Reuse bath water to water the plants.

3 Take a shorter shower and turn it off while you soap up.

4 Reuse a drinking glass all day to avoid washing too many dishes.

DON'T
THROW AWAY
THE LITTLE
CUTOUT BITS!
Use them to make
seed paper.

Make a raindrop mobile to remind you how precious water is

1 Cut out the drop shapes above and fold them all in half.

2 Make the glue on the cover flap. Glue the top side of one drop.

3 Stick another drop on top. Keep gluing and sticking all the drops.

4 Open it up, sticking the top and bottom flaps together.

5 Sew a piece of thread to the top and hang it up.

DON'T THROW THIS AWAY! Save the instructions to make more precious raindrop mobiles from recycled paper.

BUY LESS PLASTIC
to stop polluting our planet

22

Turn over to make a plastic-free gift bag.

One hundred million plastic bottles are sold each day. It can take them 1,000 years to break down. What happens to them?

Most plastic ends up littering the planet. Only a tiny amount is recycled.

Plastic in the ocean can form gigantic garbage "islands."

Around 80% is buried in landfill or dumped on land or at sea.

Just 8% of plastic is recycled.

About 12% is burnt, releasing harmful gases.

Make a plastic-free gift bag

1 Turn over to cut out the bag paper. Fold it in half, leaving a strip down the side.

2 Make the eco-friendly glue on the back cover flap. Glue the strip.

3 Fold the strip over so it glues back onto the page. Press it down.

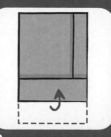

4 Fold a flap up at the bottom, at least 1 inch (3 cm) deep.

5 Fold down a triangle on each side of the flap.

6 Unfold the triangle corners again.

7 Open up the base and tuck the corners inside.

8 Fold up a small flap from the bottom.

9 Fold the top over and glue it to the bottom flap.

10 Open up the bag and pop in a gift!

DON'T THROW THIS AWAY! Save the instructions to make more gift bags from recycled paper.

THROW A SEEDBALL
to reseed the landscape

23
Turn over to make seed writing paper.

When land is cleared to build towns and cities, nature can disappear. Help bring back wildlife by planting wildflowers from seedballs.

The ball feeds the seeds, which then root into the soil.

The roots of flowers keep the soil secure so that when it rains, the soil doesn't wash away.

You will need

water

flour

dirt

native wildflower seeds

Make seedballs

1 Use a spoon to mix together two cups of dirt and half a cup of flour.

2 Slowly add about half a cup of water to bind it, like dough. Roll it into balls.

3 Roll the balls in a tray of seeds that you have collected from your local area.

4 Throw a seedball onto a bare patch of land. With rain and sun, it will grow!

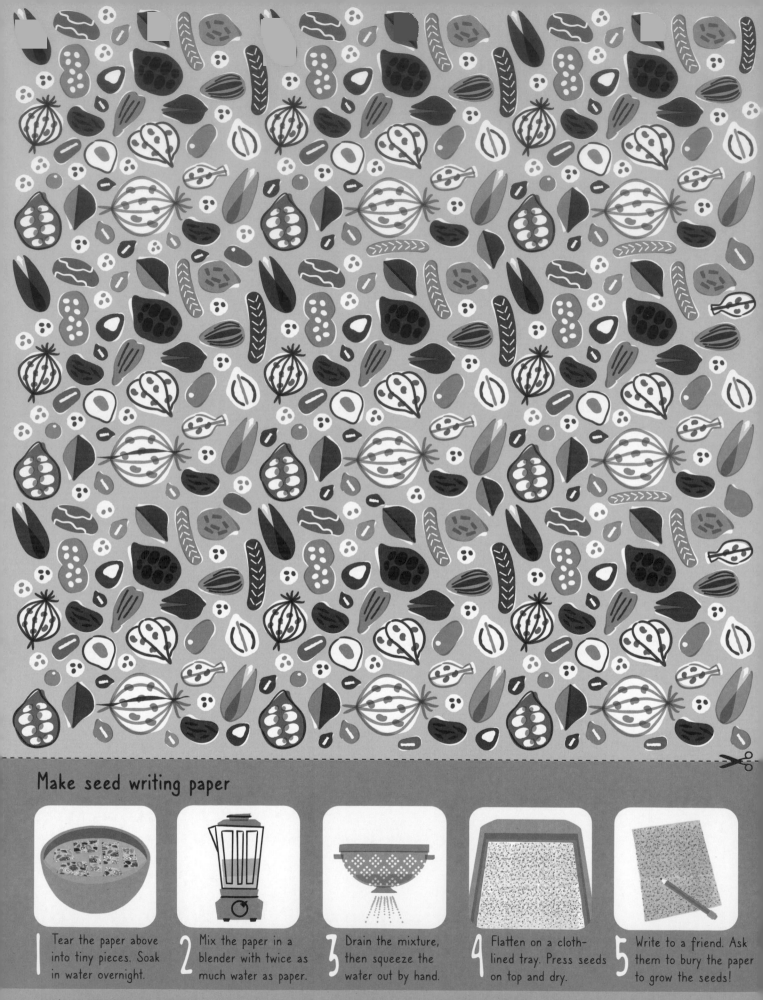

Make seed writing paper

1. Tear the paper above into tiny pieces. Soak in water overnight.

2. Mix the paper in a blender with twice as much water as paper.

3. Drain the mixture, then squeeze the water out by hand.

4. Flatten on a cloth-lined tray. Press seeds on top and dry.

5. Write to a friend. Ask them to bury the paper to grow the seeds!

DON'T THROW THIS AWAY! Keep the instructions to make more seed writing paper. Use all the little cutout bits that are leftover from this book.

MAKE A DIFFERENCE

in your own home

You can save energy all day, every day! Each bit you save will help to reduce global warming.

Unplug the computer when you are not using it.

Switch to energy-saving light bulbs.

Switch the lights off when you leave the room.

Take a shower instead of a bath.

Turn the heating off and put on a sweater!

Dry clothes outside instead of using a tumble dryer.

Play the energy hero game

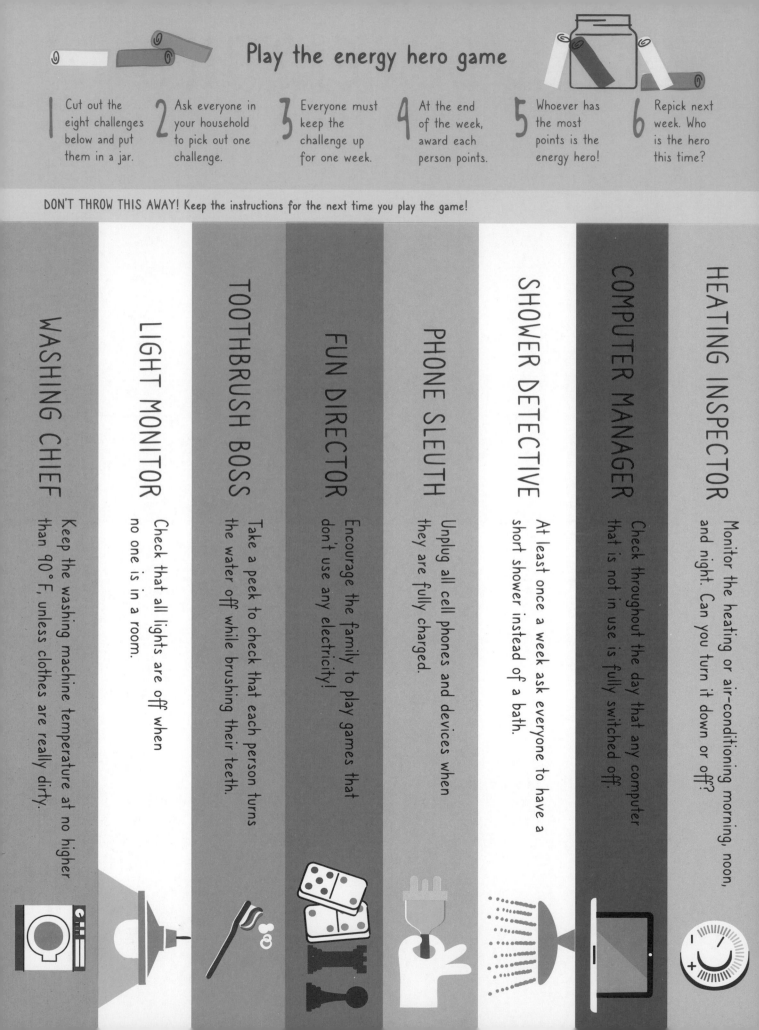

1. Cut out the eight challenges below and put them in a jar.

2. Ask everyone in your household to pick out one challenge.

3. Everyone must keep the challenge up for one week.

4. At the end of the week, award each person points.

5. Whoever has the most points is the energy hero!

6. Repick next week. Who is the hero this time?

DON'T THROW THIS AWAY! Keep the instructions for the next time you play the game!

HEATING INSPECTOR

Monitor the heating or air-conditioning morning, noon, and night. Can you turn it down or off?

COMPUTER MANAGER

Check throughout the day that any computer that is not in use is fully switched off.

SHOWER DETECTIVE

At least once a week ask everyone to have a short shower instead of a bath.

PHONE SLEUTH

Unplug all cell phones and devices when they are fully charged.

FUN DIRECTOR

Encourage the family to play games that don't use any electricity!

TOOTHBRUSH BOSS

Take a peek to check that each person turns the water off while brushing their teeth.

LIGHT MONITOR

Check that all lights are off when no one is in a room.

WASHING CHIEF

Keep the washing machine temperature at no higher than 90°F, unless clothes are really dirty.

RESCUE OLD CLOTHES
to reuse the fabric

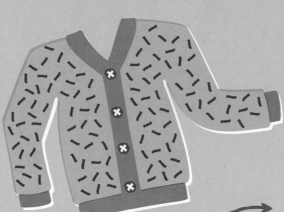

1 Don't throw away your old button-up sweater or top!

2 Cut the front and back into two squares the same size.

If you can't repair or reuse clothes, fashion them into something completely new!

3 Pin the squares together with the fronts inside and buttoned together.

4 Sew the edges together with a thick thread or yarn.

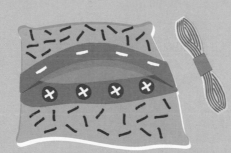

5 Open the buttons and turn the cushion inside out.

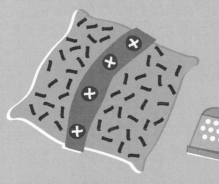

6 Stuff the cushion with other old clothes and close the buttons.

Turn your worn-out clothes into a rag rug

1 Turn over to cut out the loom. Snip the slits at the top and the bottom.

2 Cut up old scraps of fabric into ½ inch. (1 cm) wide strips.

3 Knot the strips together into one long strip.

4 Thread the strip through each slit, from top to bottom, front to back.

5 Weave a different strip of fabric from side to side, under and over.

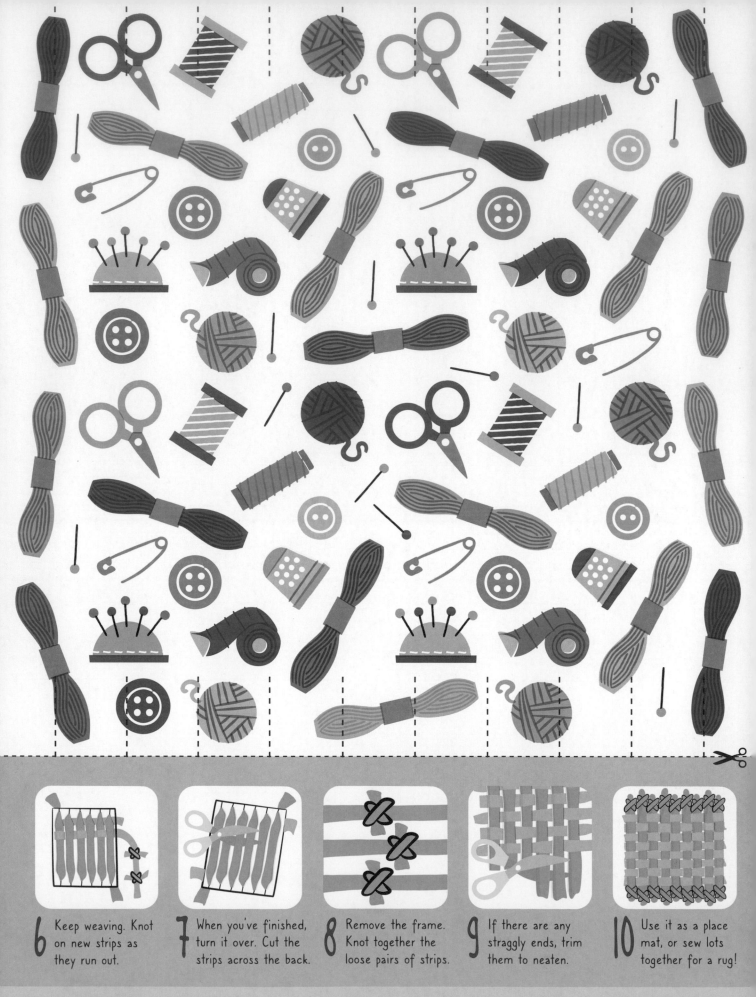

6 Keep weaving. Knot on new strips as they run out.

7 When you've finished, turn it over. Cut the strips across the back.

8 Remove the frame. Knot together the loose pairs of strips.

9 If there are any straggly ends, trim them to neaten.

10 Use it as a place mat, or sew lots together for a rug!

DON'T THROW THIS AWAY! Save the instructions to make more looms out of recycled card.

MAKE YOUR OWN PIZZA
without chemicals or food miles

26
Turn over to make an eco-friendly pizza

Cook an eco-friendly pizza from scratch. That way you save food miles, go organic, and it tastes great too!

Share your eco-pizza with a friend.

Go organic by growing fruits and vegetables without chemical pesticides.

You will need

2 pots

growing stick

onion, pepper, basil, chives, thyme, and oregano seeds

tomato plant

compost

Grow your own pizza sauce

1 Repot the tomato plant into a large container. Add a stick for it to grow up.

2 Plant the seeds. Put your pots in a sunny spot and water regularly.

3 If possible, introduce a ladybug. It will eat the pests that eat the plants!

4 After 6 to 8 weeks, harvest the fully grown plants to make pizza sauce.

Bake an organic pizza

Use your homegrown harvest to make fresh pizza sauce!
If you can, buy organic, locally made bread and cheese, too.
Ask an adult to help you to follow the steps below.

Ingredients

2 peppers

1 onion

½ cup of chopped basil,
chives, thyme, and oregano

cheese

1 small baguette

2 tsp oil

8 to 10 tomatoes

1 Ask for help to chop the onions, peppers, and tomatoes into chunks. Chop the herbs to fill half a cup.

2 Grate enough cheese to fill half a cup and leave it to one side. Preheat the oven to 450°F.

3 Ask an adult to help you heat the oil and onion in a pan. Cook for two minutes on medium heat.

4 Add the tomatoes, peppers, and herbs to the pan and stir on medium heat for 12 to 15 minutes.

5 Spread the sauce on half a baguette and sprinkle lots of cheese on top.

6 Put the baguette into the oven for 10 minutes or until the cheese melts. Ask an adult to help you take it out.

DON'T THROW THIS AWAY! Save the recipe card.

AVOID PLASTIC
to stop harming our animals

27
Turn over to make the eco flip flapper game.

Plastic can smell, taste, or even look like food to animals. When they eat it, plastic can be deadly.

Popped balloons have ended up in the bellies of kangaroos.

Elephants and other animals sometimes eat plastic waste.

Squirrels, and other small animals, get their heads stuck in tubs, trying to reach food.

Look after your pets. Sharp plastic can cut their paws.

Try the flip flapper eco-quiz

1 Turn over to make a flip flapper. To start the quiz, ask a friend to pick a number.

2 Push open and pull apart the flip flapper as many times as the number chosen.

3 Ask your friend to choose an animal that they can see.

4 Open the flip flapper under the animal chosen to find the question and answer.

5 If they answer correctly, they can have another go. If not, it's your turn.

Numbers around edge: 1, 2, 3, 4, 5, 6, 7, 8

Name three land animals that are harmed by plastic.
Possible answers: Elephants, seabirds, bears, kangaroos, squirrels, badgers, dogs, and other pets.

How long does it take plastic to break down?
Answer: It can take up to 1,000 years.

Is it OK to use plastic straws?
Answer: No. Plastic straws are used once, then thrown away. Every day millions are used—that's a lot of plastic pollution.

Name three ways you can use less plastic.
Possible answers: Avoid using plastic bottles, straws, bags, and toothbrushes. Avoid buying food in plastic packaging.

What can you use instead of a plastic shopping bag?
Possible answers: Use a canvas, paper, or cotton bag that you can either use again or recycle.

Can you think of two ocean creatures that are harmed by plastic?
Possible answers: Turtles, seals, whales, dolphins, penguins, fish, or crabs.

How do you pack a plastic-free picnic?
Answer: Buy no food with plastic packaging. Pack the food into reusable pots and use reusable bottles, plates, containers, and cutlery.

What can you use instead of a plastic toothbrush?
Answer: A bamboo toothbrush, which is natural and breaks down easily.

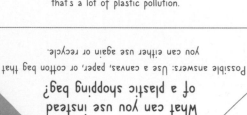

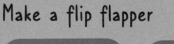

Make a flip flapper

1. Cut out the page above. Fold the paper from corner to corner.

2. Fold all four corners to the center so they reach the middle.

3. Turn over and fold each corner to the center again.

4. Fold in half both ways and unfold to loosen the flaps.

5. Tuck a finger and thumb beneath each flap to play the game!

DON'T THROW ME AWAY! Use the instructions to make more flip flapper games and eco-quizzes with recycled paper.

EAT UP
to stop food waste

28

Turn over to cook up your leftovers.

A third of the world's food is thrown away. Food waste in landfill releases poisonous gases that heat up the air, increasing global warming.

Many people don't have enough food, so don't waste it!

It takes a lot of energy, water, and farmland to produce food.

Waste less food in your home

1 Try not to buy, cook, or put on your plate more food than you really need.

2 Buy less food by growing your own. There will be less plastic packaging too.

3 Don't throw away your odd-shaped vegetables. They taste just as good.

4 Compost vegetable and fruit peelings instead of putting them in landfill.

5 Don't throw away food unless it has gone bad.

French toast

Ingredients

2 slices of bread—they can be a bit stale, but not moldy.

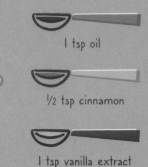

I tsp oil

½ tsp cinnamon

I tsp vanilla extract

I egg

¼ cup milk

1. Crack the egg into a bowl and whisk it to mix it up.

2. Pour in the milk, cinnamon, and vanilla, and whisk until it is all mixed in.

3. Dip the bread into the mixture. Make sure both sides are covered.

4. Pour the oil into a pan. Ask an adult to help fry the bread on both sides until golden.

Ripe banana pancakes

Ingredients

½ cup plain yogurt

I tbsp oil

I egg

I ripe banana

I tbsp honey

I cup oats

syrup

a handful of blueberries

1. Put the yogurt, banana, oats, egg, and honey into a blender and blend.

2. Ask an adult to heat a little oil in a pan and pour in some of the batter.

3. When the pancake begins to bubble, ask an adult to flip it. Fry until golden brown.

4. Serve with a drizzle of syrup, blueberries, and a few banana slices.

SPREAD THE WORD
to help save the planet

29 Turn over to wear and share eco badges

Everyone needs to help when it comes to saving the planet. But even little actions can make a BIG difference. Shout loudly and get everyone involved!

Reduce, reuse, and recycle!

Plant a tree . . . or two!

Protect wild animals!

Compost food waste!

Upcycle clothes and junk!

Save water and power!

Sow wildflower seeds!

Make badges to pass on your message

1 Cut out the badge bases from the inside back cover of this book.

2 Turn this page over to find the badge fronts. Cut them out.

3 Make your own eco-friendly glue to stick them on.

4 Fasten a safety pin to the back with eco-friendly tape.

5 Wear your badge with pride, or give it to a friend!

Save the bees!

recycle me

Adopt a tiger

bring back wildflowers

Save our oceans!

go green
go cycling

Save energy

Be a litter hero!

Save water

recycle, recycle, recycle

Save our trees

Say NO to plastic!

help bees, plant seeds

Stop food waste!

make compost, not landfill

make friends with a bug

go organic

adopt a polar bear

cut plastic, save ocean creatures

go green, grow your own

Plant a Tree
Save the Earth

DON'T THROW AWAY THE LITTLE CUTOUT BITS! Use them for your bug hotel or to make seed paper.